ALL YOU NEED TO KNOW ABOUT MAKING MONEY ONLINE

A COMPLETE BLUEPRINT

BY

JAMES F BASS

CHAPTER 7 TIPS FOR MANAGING FINANCES AND SCALING YOUR ONLINE BUSINESS

CONCLUSION

This is 'All You Need to Know About Making Money Online: A Complete Blueprint', a comprehensive guide that aims to empower you with the knowledge, strategies, and tools to thrive in the ever-evolving world of online money-making. In this digital era, the internet has opened up unprecedented opportunities for individuals to generate income from the comfort of their own homes. Whether you're seeking financial freedom, additional income, or the flexibility of working on your terms, this book is your ultimate resource to navigate the vast online landscape and achieve your financial goals.

We understand that the realm of making money online can be daunting and overwhelming, especially for beginners. With countless opportunities, scams, and misinformation floating around, it can be challenging to know where to start and who to trust. This is where 'All You Need to Know About Making Money Online: A Complete Blueprint' comes in. We have compiled all the essential information, strategies, and tips you need to successfully establish and grow a profitable online income stream.

The blueprint outlined in this book is designed to provide you with a structured framework that eliminates guesswork and maximizes your chances of success. Whether you are a novice with no prior experience or a seasoned online entrepreneur looking to diversify your income, this guide caters to individuals of all skill levels. We firmly believe that anyone, with the right knowledge and determination, can tap into the vast potential of making money online.

Throughout this comprehensive guide, we will cover a wide range of essential topics, including:

1. Understanding the Online Ecosystem: We will delve into the dynamics of the online world, exploring the various avenues and opportunities available for generating income. From e-commerce and dropshipping to digital marketing and affiliate programs, we will provide an overview of the different paths you can explore.

2. Choosing the Right Online Business Model: We will guide you through the process of identifying the online business model that aligns with your skills, interests, and goals. Each model comes with its own

set of advantages, challenges, and revenue streams, and we will help you make an informed decision.

3. Setting Up Your Online Presence: Creating a strong online presence is crucial for success in the digital realm. We will guide you through the process of setting up your website, optimizing it for search engines, and establishing a strong social media presence. Additionally, we will explore the importance of branding and building trust with your audience.

4. Monetizing Your Online Presence: Once you have established your online presence, it's time to monetize it effectively. We will explore various monetization strategies, such as advertising, sponsored content, selling digital products, and offering online services. You will gain insights into choosing the right revenue streams and maximizing your earning potential.

5. Driving Traffic to Your Online Platforms: The key to success in the online world lies in driving quality traffic to your platforms. We will delve into the world of digital marketing, exploring the strategies and techniques to attract and engage your target audience. From search engine optimization (SEO) and content marketing to social media advertising and email marketing, we will equip you with the necessary tools to boost your online visibility.

6. Scaling and Growing Your Online Business: Once you have established a successful online income stream, the journey doesn't stop there. We will explore strategies to scale and grow your business, including automation, outsourcing, expanding your product or service offerings, and diversifying your revenue streams. We believe in continually evolving and adapting to maximize your success in the long run.

In addition to these core topics, 'All You Need to Know About Making Money Online: A Complete Blueprint' also includes real-life case studies, and actionable tips to provide you with a comprehensive and well-rounded understanding of online money-making. I believe that learning from the experiences and successes of others can be invaluable in your own online journey.

My goal with this book is to empower you with the knowledge, tools, and confidence to tap into the vast potential of making money online. Whether you dream of financial freedom, additional income streams, or the flexibility to work on your terms, this blueprint is designed to help you achieve those aspirations. So, get ready to embark on an exciting journey of exploration, growth, and financial empowerment. We are thrilled to be your companions on this path to online success.

Remember, making money online is not a get-rich-quick scheme. It requires dedication, persistence, and continuous learning. However, with the right mindset and the information provided in this blueprint, you have everything you need to establish a successful online income stream. Let's dive in and unlock the limitless possibilities of making money online!

The Future Of
Online Marketplace

Voice Command Searching

Inclusion of Vertical Marketplace

Rise of Brick and Click Policy

The Introduction of Recommerce

Popular Mobile Shopping

AI Technology for Constant Service

Omni-Channel is the New Trend

Online retail has considerably evolved with the advent of dropshipping. As a painless and low-capital way to get involved in e-commerce, dropshipping gives aspiring entrepreneurs a gateway to business success through platforms like Alibaba.com.

If you're new to dropshipping, you may still be trying to work out the basics of this e-commerce strategy and how to apply it to your business. Not to worry, you're in the right place.

The movements of the prices in global, regional or local markets are captured in price indices called stock market indices, of which there are many, e.g. the S&P, the FTSE, the Euronext indices and the NIFTY & SENSEX of India. Such indices are usually market capitalization weighted, with the weights reflecting the contribution of the stock to the index. The constituents of the index are reviewed frequently to include/exclude stocks in order to reflect the changing business environment.

Derivative Instruments

Financial innovation has brought many new financial instruments whose pay-offs or values depend on the prices of stocks. Some examples are exchange-traded funds (ETFs), stock index and stock options, equity swaps, single-stock futures, and stock index futures. These last two may be traded on futures exchanges which are distinct from stock exchanges; their history traces back to commodity futures exchanges, or traded over the counter. As all of these products are only derived from stocks, they are sometimes considered to be traded in a hypothetical derivatives market, rather than the hypothetical stock market.

Leverage strategy

Stock that a trader does not actually own may be traded using short selling; margin buying may be used to purchase stock with borrowed funds; or, derivatives may be used to control large blocks of stocks for a much smaller amount of money than would be required by outright purchase or sales.

Short selling

In short selling, the trader borrows stock (usually from his brokerage which holds its clients shares or its own shares on account to lend to short sellers) then sells it on the market, betting that the price will fall. The trader eventually buys back the stock, making money if the price fell in the meantime and losing money if it rose. Exiting a short position by buying back the stock is called "covering". This strategy may also be used by unscrupulous traders in illiquid or thinly traded markets to artificially lower the price of a stock. Hence most markets either prevent short selling or place restrictions on when and how a short sale can occur. The practice of naked shorting is illegal in most (but not all) stock markets.

Margin buying

In margin buying, the trader borrows money (at interest) to buy a stock and hopes for it to rise. Most industrialized countries have regulations that require that if the borrowing is based on collateral from other stocks the trader owns outright, it can be a maximum of a certain percentage of those other stocks' value. In the United States, the margin requirements have been 50% for many years (that is, if you want to make a $1000 investment, you need to put up $500, and there is often a maintenance margin below the $500).

A margin call is made if the total value of the investor's account cannot support the loss of the trade. Upon a decline in the value of the margined securities additional funds may be required to maintain the account's equity, and with or without notice the margined security or any others within the account may be sold by the brokerage to protect its loan position. The investor is responsible for any shortfall following such forced sales.

Regulation of margin requirements (by the Federal Reserve) was implemented after the Crash of 1929. Before that, speculators typically only needed to put up as little as 10 percent (or even less) of the total investment represented by the stocks purchased. Other rules may include the prohibition of free-riding: putting in an order to buy stocks without paying initially (there is normally a three-day grace period for delivery of the stock), but then selling them (before the three-days are up) and using part of the proceeds to make the original payment assuming that the value of the stocks has not declined in the interim.

Types of financial market

Financial markets can be divided into different subtypes:

For the assets transferred
- Money market : It is traded with money or financial assets with short-term maturity and high liquidity, generally assets with a term of less than one year.
- Capital market : Financial assets with medium and long-term maturity are traded, which are

basic for carrying out certain investment processes.

Depending on its structure

- Organized market
- Non-organized markets denominated in English (" Over The Counter ").

According to the negotiation phase of financial assets

- Primary market : Financial assets are created. In this market, assets are transmitted directly by their issuer.
- Secondary market : Only existing financial assets are exchanged, which were issued at a previous time. This market allows holders of financial assets to sell instruments that were already issued in the primary market (or that had already been transmitted in the secondary market) and that are in their possession, or to buy other financial assets.

According to the geographical perspective

- National markets. The currency in which the financial assets are denominated and the residence of those involved is national.
- International markets. The markets are situated outside a country's geographical area.

According to the type of asset traded

- Traditional market. In which financial assets such as demand deposits, stocks or bonds are traded.
- Alternative market. In which alternative financial assets are traded such as portfolio investments, promissory notes, factoring, real estate (e.g. through fiduciary rights), in private equity funds, venture capital funds, hedge funds, investment

projects (e.g. infrastructure, cinema, etc.) among many others.

Other markets

- Commodity markets, which allow the trading of commodities
- Derivatives markets, which provide instruments for managing financial risk
- Forward markets, which provide standardized forward contracts to trade products at a future date
- Insurance markets, which allows the redistribution of varied risks
- Foreign exchange market, which allows the exchange of foreign currencies

Investment Strategy

Many strategies can be classified as either fundamental analysis or technical analysis. Fundamental analysis refers to analyzing companies by their financial statements found in SEC filings, business trends, and general economic conditions. Technical analysis studies price actions in markets through the use of charts and quantitative techniques to attempt to forecast price trends based on historical performance, regardless of the company's financial prospects. One example of a technical strategy is the Trend following method, used by John W. Henry and Ed Seykota, which uses price patterns and is also rooted in risk management and diversification.

Additionally, many choose to invest via passive index funds. In this method, one holds a portfolio of the entire stock market or some segment of the stock market (such as the S&P 500 Index or Wilshire 5000). The principal aim of this strategy is to maximize diversification, minimize taxes from realizing gains, and ride the general trend of the stock market to rise.

Responsible investment emphasizes and requires a long-term horizon on the basis of fundamental analysis only, avoiding hazards in the expected return of the investment. Socially responsible investing is another investment preference.

Taxation

Taxation is a consideration of all investment strategies; profit from owning stocks, including dividends received, is subject to different tax rates depending on the type of security and the holding period. Most profit from stock investing is taxed via a capital gains tax. In many countries, the corporations pay taxes to the government and the shareholders once again pay taxes when they profit from owning the stock, known as "double taxation".